# PRAYVOLUTION

# PRAYVOLUTION

## START YOUR PRAYER REVOLUTION TODAY!

JEROME J. CASE

MAXIM DART PUBLISHING
DECATUR, GEORGIA

Request for Information: www.jeromejcase.com
Cover Design: Kenosis Design Innovations

# DEDICATION

*Dedicated in the loving memory of my determined and amazing mother, Ms. Willie M. Sawyer. Watching you seize the courage and freedom that comes from the power and authority of prayer while battling drug addiction and cancer still inspires me.*

# CONTENTS

# TESTIMONIALS

"Given the times that we are living in, everyone needs a serious prayer life, not only to survive, but to thrive. Jerome Case, in his own unique way, has given us a powerful guide to prayer through the use of his own soul-stirring prayers. This book of prayers, from the heart of a man who loves God and clearly enjoys talking to God, will revolutionize your prayer life and your prayers will help transform our world."

**Cynthia L. Hale**
Senior Pastor
Ray of Hope Christian Church, Decatur, GA

"Prayer changes things! This is no doubt the understatement of the year coming from one whose life had been so profoundly changed by prayer as mine has been. This most readable book on the discipline of prayer provides a glimpse of the power available to each of us to change ourselves and others through heartfelt, honest conversation with our Father. It's not only a "how-to" manual, but it's a treasure trove of actual prayers that can easily be co-opted into the reader's own personal situations and circumstances. This book is for anyone who desires to grow their own prayer life while simultaneously experiencing the didactic interchange that occurs when the heart of the made connects with the heart of the Maker!"

**Bishop Carl McRae**
Founding Pastor
Exousia Lighthouse Christian Ministries, Lithonia, GA
Author, Returning to God with your Whole Heart:
A Beginners Guide to Fasting

"I found myself mesmerized by the beauty of the text. Mr. Case eloquently illustrated the need for an authentic relationship with God. In addition, the stories shared showed his vulnerability allowing the reader to be vulnerable as well. The repetitive steps for prayer seemed simplistic at first, yet engaging. Each allowed me to create a sincere prayer full of my true desires. My prayer life has been strengthened by his book."

**Jaye Lynn Peabody, MPA, M.DIV., MS, LPC, NCC**
Psychotherapist, The Peabody Practice, LLC
Executive Pastor, New Bethel AME Church

"Prayvolution is a prayerfully and divinely orchestrated resource that has the potential to transform the way we think, approach and engage in prayer. The prayers offered are theologically powerful. I cannot wait to add this to our recommended reading list."

**Rev. Dr. Nathaniel Dunlap, Jr.**
Executive Director & Chairman
The PRF Teaching Ministry

"Prayvolution is not your typical book of prayers. It is a book that pulls you in with the reality of life and comforts you with the treasure of the Word of God. From the Pearls of Big Momma's wisdom to the faithful prayers of a praying Grandma, and on to the reminder of joy in every area of life and freedom beyond your past. Prayvolution is truly a revolution of Prayer. Every Apostle, Prophet, Evangelist, Pastor and Teacher should have this book in their library. Peace & Blessings."

**Chris Brunson**
International Recording Artist

"In Prayvolution, Elder Jerome Case has forged from the fiery passion of his heart an invaluable jewel for the body of Christ, a collection of spirit-filled prayers that are guaranteed to draw Christians in to a closer relationship with God. If you desire to develop a deeper and more meaningful prayer life with God, Prayvolution will equip and empower you to do so. Trust me, I know from first-hand experience!"

**Kewon Foster**
Church Planter /Pastor
Out of Love Ministries

"Prayer is establishing a relationship with God. Case, using himself as an example, lays out an amazing guide to help people dissect and understand prayer conversations. This is a vital read for new and seasoned Christians."

**Taunya A. Lowe, Ph.D.**
CEO & Chief Riot Starter
DrTaunyaLowe.com

"Prayvolution is an acknowledgement that the most powerful starting point of all change is our hearts and minds. With these inspired daily prayers and reflections, Case offers us practical steps into the discipline and delights of daily prayer. Yes, these particular pathways are anchored in his narrative, voice and experiences, but Case offers them as a beginning (not an end) to our own self-styled prayer life. Prayvolution's structure and form reminds us that prayer is a daily commitment from which all meaningful growth and lasting change is anchored. I commend this powerful resource to you as you open a new chapter of depth and meaning in your relationship with God."

**C. Milano// Harden**
Chief Executive
C.MILANO//Inc. Metro Atlanta, GA

"Prayer is a powerful gift given to us by God. This book will help you make use of the gift of prayer through a structured, simple, and dynamic approach. Prayvolution is a must-read, must-have, and must share."

**Shawn Robinson**
Founder & President
Orange Arrow

"Prayvolution is a dynamic journal that allows individuals to tap into their inner strength and relationship with God on a higher level. It is a beautiful tool that believers can look back and reflect upon as they build their faith and the self-discipline to conquer life's challenges as well as embrace its beautiful rewards!"

**Jennifer Hopson**
CEO, Author, & Motivational Speaker
Dill Purple Geniuses Media

"Bernard McGinn defines Christian mysticism as "that part, or element, of Christian belief and practice that concerns the preparation for, the consciousness, and the effect of a direct and transformative presence of God." Prayvolution accomplishes the journey to an encounter with God through reflection, prayer, and self-examination. In the early church, great thinkers like St. Jerome, St. Augustine of Hippo and the late American Theologian Dr. Howard Thurman were proponents of Christian thinking and spiritual preparation. After reading Prayvolution, we can celebrate Elder Jerome Case as a new addition to the list of great thinkers, as he captivates us through prayer, practice, and reflection. Prayvolution is a must have book for every believer."

**Rev. Keith Jamal Hammond M.Div.**
Author, Built To Be Broken
Assoc. Pastor, Mt. Carmel Baptist Church

# INTRODUCTION

*But seek first his kingdom and his righteousness, and all things will be given to you as well. — Matthew 6:33*

During the days of sunshine, blue skies, happiness, joy, and peace, it's easy for us to stretch out in the green meadows of success, lay our heads back on the folds of our accomplishments and stare out into the horizon contemplating endless possibilities. In the good times of life, everything seems right, balanced, and in order. Our little worlds of self-contained faith appear to orbit around God's shining favor, and we feel like every idea and dream is achievable.

But as soon as the sudden storms of life roll in and drench our mental portraits of a glorious sun-shining day, our attitudes and positions of faith change. All of a sudden happiness turns into frustration, joy turns into depression, and peace becomes doubt. Why?

Because for too many Christians, the roots of their faith don't go deep enough to stabilize them during the storms of life. In trying times, a lot of believers fall apart, unable to access the required depths of secure faith, because their prayer life hasn't gone beyond the surface of a loose and casual relationship with God. As a result, some believers don't know how to access the power of God that can only be attained through the power of relational prayers. So they miss out on experiencing the supply of God's divine dew falling and saturating their situations.

When there is no consistent communication with God, there can be no real relationship with Him. As a result, your faith is only cultivated in the soil of a shallow prayer life. At times your faith may feel strong, but it can be blown away with ease when unexpected tornadoes spiral in because your relationship with God hasn't been adequately cultivated through your words – your prayers. As a result, your faith crumbles quickly because you don't know how to access the throne room of the Lord so that you can lift the proper petitions to His ears.

1 John 5:14-15 says, *"This is the confidence we have in approaching God: that if we ask anything according to his will, he hears us. And if we know that he hears us — whatever we ask — we know that we have what we asked of him."*

Often when we make an attempt to pray, we're not sure if God hears us or if He's even listening. So we doubt the power of prayer. We doubt God's love for us. We become jaded. We become frustrated. We take on an attitude of dismissiveness. But that's due to our lack of sustained effort to cultivate a rich meaningful and communal relationship with God.

Don't you want a meaningful and powerful prayer life? Absolutely! You want a prayer life that is profound and fulfilling. You want to be the kind of person who's able to traverse the valleys and oceans of life's challenges with secure confidence. You want to have the kind of faith that is ordered by prayer and sees the fruits of your folded hands manifest miracles so that you'll be able to navigate situations by the wise unction of God. When evil comes, or someone becomes terribly sick and dies, the hurricanes of life won't overtake your faith, because you know that God will hear your prayers. You know that whatever you ask, you'll have what you've requested from Him. Your confidence will be built on a solid relationship with God that has been nurtured, protected and valued.

But how do you develop the kind of meaningful relationship with God that will lead to an effective and powerful prayer life? There are a few ways: Setting aside daily time with God, being intentional about talking to God, being completely transparent about everything in your life, and writing out your prayers.

If you're not spending quality prayer time with God daily, you're going to have a dry and unfulfilled prayer life. You won't be able to handle the slings and arrows of the enemy. But if you're serious, and you desire to communicate with God on a new and dynamic level, then you'll have to sit still sometimes, be quiet sometimes, walk around sometimes, and even get loud sometimes as you let the power of prayer move you. But most of all, you'll need to read the Bible, listen to the Holy Sprit's guidance, and journal your prayers. Only then, as your prayer life grows stronger, will you witness an amazing transformation take place. Soon, ordinary conversations with God will lead to that deeper spiritual connection in your faith. And shortly after you'll find yourself able to access a level of praying faith that can overcome every situation inside of every storm. A prayer life that is ready to support your spiritual revolution, ready to embrace a Prayvolution!

**So why did I write this book? Why did I want to share my own prayers with the world?**

Well I'm glad that you asked. And the answer is simple. I was burning in my bones and I had to get it out. I was tired of seeing people that the Triune God called to be change-agents in the world, unable to pray for others and even for themselves. I wanted to do something to help break the yoke of poor praying habits and to destroy the chains of intimidation when it comes to praying publically. That's when I decided to yield to the calling of this book.

So, on the morning of October 21, 2015, I awoke with an inspired determination to finally write a powerful book that was entirely composed of my personal prayers. Early in the wee hours of the morning, the spirit of urgency captured me, and I felt as though God was prompting me to start pulling together prayers that I had written over the past twelve years. I felt the Holy Spirit declaring that I needed to share these God-given prayers with the world.

There was no more time to delay. There were no more excuses. And there were no more justifiable limitations or barriers. The circumstances surrounding my life were not going to change, but I could change how I responded to the events and how I allowed them to affect my confidence about wring this book. So, I took charge of the negativity in my mind, and when I set my feet on the floor that morning, and started declaring that this prayer book was going to happen. I declared that it was going to help somebody.

After standing up and taking a deep breath, the first thing I did was get my mind ready to talk to God about this prayer book that He planted in my spirit. Then, I made a conscientious effort to get my heart and body into a position of submission and started praying to God for vision and guidance. I began talking to God and listening to His directions, and I could feel the revolution happening within my spirit. With every transparent word framed by surrender, adoration, confession and thanksgiving, I could feel the act of prayer winning and knew that the spirit of doubt was defeated.

See, for years I wanted to write a book about prayer. I wanted to share the spiritual inspiration and motivational messages that God provided to me with the world. I wanted to share our intimate conversations, but I found and embraced every excuse that prevented me from achieving my goal. I agreed with every distraction that took me off the desired path. I allowed myself to become trapped in a mental prison of doubt, and I was the co-warden with the Devil. Because up until that intentional moment, that intimate quite-time of transparent conversation, that sacred prayer time, I had permitted an already defeated enemy to cloud my vision about writing a life-changing book for the people who needed a personal, spiritual prison break. But October 21, 2015 was the day I started a personal prayer revolution, and God promised me that He would be my supply, banner, shield, and guide. He heard my sincere prayer petition. In fact, I believe that He was waiting on my prayer to shift the undesirable atmosphere that had I had created over the years. God was expecting for me to arrive at the realization that I was the hindrance to the gift that He had planted in my heart when I first desired to write a book concerning prayer years ago.

Please understand, my prayer life is everything to me. I know that it sounds cliché, but when I think about every positive transformative experience that I have had as a Christian, prayer was always the starting point. Every time I prepared my spirit for the inevitable negative vicissitudes of life, I was able to overcome them all because I was "prayed up". And when you're intentionally prayed up, then you can see the opposition coming, you're able to withstand every attack, and you're ready to speak life into dead situations. You're capable of breaking down barriers, overcoming obstacles, and standing firm knowing that God will honor your prayerful request.

I believe that having a submitted and committed relationship to God along with an active daily prayer life is the key to unlocking the rich saturation of God's will and promises for our lives. Remember, honest prayer is an authentic and transparent act of humility. So when we humble ourselves and turn to God, He is willing to hear our hearts in heaven and respond to our faintest petition.

Just like any loving parental relationship, our Father, who is in heaven, is always seeking and wanting to know what His child needs. The Lord, our God is the ultimate father, seeking the ultimate conversation with His children. Thus, prayer is one of the greatest relationship tools God has given to humanity and those of us that have received the covenant of Salvation through Christ Jesus. The act of prayer in itself is an activity of the Covenant of Grace that enables us to freely communicate about everything with God. Being in covenant with God and talking to Him while praying is like offering up a sweet aroma of loving trust and a pleasant fragrance of faith.

The activity of prayer is a powerful resource because it provides us with the opportunity to express our truest needs and beliefs to a Father who is bent towards earth listening for the words of faith. Prayer allows us to seek God's intimate guidance and will for our lives. Praying to God enables believers to intercede on the behalf of others. Petitioning God can heal sicknesses, destroy diseases, break emotional strongholds, eliminate financial burdens, and overcome social injustices. Also, prayer is the most efficient and effective supernatural way to cast out the demonic while defeating the plans of the enemy.

When we consider the practice of praying daily, we must understand that our faith is the foundational binding agent of our prayer life. In addition, we must realize that our prayer life is like the nutrition delivery agent to our faith. Since Jesus Christ is the cornerstone of the Christian faith, the bricks of our faith are set and secured by the mortar of a healthy spirituality. Our prayers won't manifest anything until we believe that the central figure of our faith is engaged or willing to act upon our prayerful request.

As Christians, it's vital that we understand that the effectiveness of our prayers is reliant on a healthy relationship with God in respect to the sinfulness that may exist in our lives. It's imperative that we willfully maintain a Christ-centered lifestyle of repentance and holiness so that our prayers to God aren't impeded by the adversarial desires of the flesh, sin or Satan. Our daily prayer life is serious business, and the activity of prayer is real work that's tied to real accomplishments, real results, real miracles, real transformations, and real testimonies.

Therefore, this book is my sincere gift of support to be added to your spiritual toolbox, backpack, and war room. It's my hope that you'll embrace the transparency of my conversations with our Triune God within these pages and that you'll be inspired, motivated, encouraged, strengthened, empowered, and lifted above every issue in your life. And it's my desire that you'll actively partner with these paragraphs of faith to discover a brighter life, deeper peace, expanded hope, needed healing, fresh renewal, inspired revival, and the power to start your prayer revolution today – your personal Prayvolution!

As you journey through these pages you'll encounter sacred moments of clarity and personal reflection. As you sojourn between the biblical verses and the connected prayers, expect to be filled with moments of genuine inspiration to talk to God in your unique way. Expect to be pulled to a quiet place within your spirit and allow the Holy Spirit to wash over you with divine feeling, divine words of comfort, direction, and confirmation. Be ready to start writing out your personal prayers. Prepare to discover your deeper voice of prayer and praise. Get ready to start turning your favorite and even random Bible verses into the serious life changing, impacting, and soul-stirring prayers. Be ready to develop crazy expectations of faith. Be ready to experience the overflow of amazing levels of new confidence. Be ready to embrace the power of transformative conviction. Be ready to feel empowered to start praying as the Holy Spirit commands. Don't be surprised when you find yourself on fire with the supernatural urge and desire to start writing all kinds of prayers for other people. Don't be surprised when you find yourself in the center of your personal Prayvolution.

Now after reading all of that, you still may be saying to yourself "I don't know how to pray well," "I don't know how to pray at all," or "I don't have time to journal my prayers." Well, don't worry. This book was created to assist with countering those kinds of feelings. This book was written with a purpose to help and inspire you while you navigate through its pages of intentional prayers. After each prayer, you'll find two questions and a space full of opportunity that has been made available for you to write your private prayer. It's a sacred space just for you.

At the end of this prayer book, it is my hope that you'll be able to look back and see how your prayers have developed and have been answered. Also, you'll witness how your prayer life has matured and grown in content as well as expectation and transparency. You'll be able to pray with power and authority. You'll be able to pray publicly with confidence. And you won't be filled with doubt about what you're praying for anymore. You'll be a four-star general in your personal Prayvolution. But most of all, you'll witness how your personal relationship with God has grown in the areas of faith, belief, trust, hope, humility, and love. You'll have such great confidence in your prayer life that the glow of being in the presence of God will be a testimony for others to witness. Your Prayvolution will be a light to others as you become a blessing of salt within your community.

**Pray this prayer with me.**

*I praise and thank you, Lord God. I thank you for seeing me through the lenses of eternity, lenses that aren't blurred by my failings and my stumbling. I thank you, Lord, for encouraging me from the vantage point of my finished destiny. I thank you, God, for your unfailing love and your unshakable support. Thank you, Lord, for seeing the best in me, even right now. And I thank you for loving me on purpose. Now please hear this humble prayer as I start this journey to building a deeper prayer life and relationship with you. I offer this prayer in the strong name of Jesus. Amen.*

# THE ROOTS OF MY PRAYERS

*The prayer of a righteous person is powerful and effective.* — James 5:13

The roots of this humble book were planted in a spiritual soil tended by two beautiful seasoned saints that helped to shape my foundational understanding concerning prayer. These two fabulous ladies were Mrs. Jeanette Sawyer and Mrs. Hanna Freeman. Both have gone to be with the Lord God in Heaven, but their memories and life lessons will always be present with me.

Mrs. Hanna Freeman was a dear friend, mentor, and confidant of my deceased mother, Mrs. Willie M. Sawyer (maiden name). As a child, I called Mrs. Hanna Freeman "Big Momma," a loving name that she earned for a good reason. Big Momma was not a petite woman in stature, personality, or presence. She had the plus size and candid attitude that commanded the attention and respect of everyone. She was old school, classy, stern, and wise. Also, God had spent extra time allowing the sun to kiss her skin, giving her a smooth dark complexion that contrasted with her extra-long flowing silver hair. I loved Big Momma because she was fun, loving, and generous.

I remember that she never listened to the radio when she drove because she always kept a hymn or gospel song on her lips. And that kind of spiritual meditation through worship is what she imparted to me. Still, what impacted me the most was her patient and step-by-step instruction when she taught me the Lord's Prayer. It was the Matthew 6:9-13 King James Version – the only version that mattered back in her day.

# PRAYVOLUTION

*Our Father, which art in heaven, Hallowed be thy name.*
*Thy kingdom come, Thy will be done in earth, as it is in heaven.*
*Give us this day our daily bread.*
*And forgive us our debts, as we forgive our debtors.*
*And lead us not into temptation, but deliver us from evil: For thine is the kingdom,*
*and the power, and the glory, for ever, Amen.*

And when I would spend the night at her house while my single mother was working at her overnight job, Big Momma would make sure that I always said the Lord's Prayer before I crawled into bed. On those nights, Big Momma would sit in a chair and say, "Pop, before you go to bed you need to kneel down, get your hands ready, and say your prayers." Afterward, she'd tuck me in, turn out the room light, and pull the door closed just enough for me to see the light from the hall.

I'll always be grateful to "Big Momma" for planting the seeds that have impacted my life and the lives of others around me. The fact is that we can never know how the seeds of our prayer life will impact or change someone else's life. And we will never know how long it will take before the seeds produce a harvest. But by faith, we can believe that a transformational harvest of abundance will be produced when we plant our lives, trust, hope, dreams, and desires into God's fertilized soil of divine promises.

The second most impactful person is my praying grandmother, Mrs. Jeanette Sawyer, who was affectionately known as "Grandma." She transitioned to the glory of Heaven on March 25, 2015, at the golden age of 91. I'm honored to celebrate her memory as a true prayer warrior and a strong woman of faith.

For the record, it was not until after I had accepted Jesus as my Lord and Savior that I began to appreciate the living example of my grandmother's faith and prayer life. Only after I had given my life to Christ as an adult did I start to understand the depth of my grandmother's prayer life and the kind of relationship that she had with God. And we grew closer because of our faith connection through Christ Jesus as my prayer life began to flourish.

Without a doubt, it's an honored blessing to be able to pray with your grandmother and to talk about the things of God on a level that no one else understands. Because of those intimate conversations and prayer with my grandmother, I learned about real faith in God, Jesus, the Holy Spirit, and faith in love. And when I became ordained, I found myself in the position of not just learning from my grandmother, but as a resource for her as a minister. But it was her testimonies about her intercessory prayers and her daily prayer life that ministered to me in times of my doubt and unbelief.

Although Grandma did not teach me the Lord's Prayer, she did teach me about having an intimate relationship with the Lord. She taught me about seeking God's face and resting on His promises. She taught me about the sacrifice of intercession and long-suffering faith. And most of all, she taught me how to keep it real with God through honest and open conversations. She would tell me, "Just talk to Jesus. Tell Him all about your issues. He's listening, son. He's listening. Just talk to Him."

And while encouraging my transparency, Grandma guided me on how to pray for the forgiveness of my enemies, to be emotionally honest in prayer, and not to be consumed by frustration with others. Also, my Grandma taught me to honor the calling on my life through prayer and to believe in God's plan for my life. And every time we talked on the phone, she would tell me how much she prayed for me and believed in me. I tell you, there's nothing like a praying grandmother that believes in your purpose in life.

And during those phone calls, my grandma would always ask me a simple question, "Did you pray for me today?" Some days I was happy to tell her 'yes' and on other days I would have to confess that I had not prayed for her. That was her way of keeping me honest about my faithfulness to my call. She knew that if I could not pray for my family, then I was not going to be able to pray for strangers. Plus, having a grandson as a minister to pray for her was a privilege for us both. And sometimes she would intentionally ask me to pray for her right after my sad confession. Then afterward, she would say, "You only prayed for me because you felt guilty, but I'll take it because at least it was a good prayer." Then, like two old buddies, we would fall out laughing together.

At the end of every phone conversation, she would affirm me and tell me that she loved me, she was praying for me, and that she wanted me to be sure to pray for her too. I must admit that I looked forward to hearing her affirmation because I knew that she was praying for me. I knew that she was covering me and that she knew that God was listening.

With that said, I'm so grateful for the two amazing women who planted their seeds of prayer, watered them, and allowed them to grow in the soil of my existence. I'm grateful to the Lord God and humbled that He blessed me with two loving souls that taught me about the power of prayer. And so I hope that this personal labor of love, faith, and transparency will find a place in your daily routine as well as a resting place in your spiritual soil so that as you grow, you'll continue the blessing forward.

# SO, WHAT IS PRAYER ALL ABOUT?

To many, prayer is some profound, enigmatic ritual. To some, prayer is a pattern of deep spiritual meditation. For others, prayer is the anchor of their religion. To a lot of people, prayer is a mystery that seems to escape logic. However, it is not incomprehensible. Still, for Christians, prayer is one of the greatest relationship blessings God has allowed humanity to receive via the gift of Salvation through the covenant of grace. The act of prayer enables believers in Jesus Christ to communicate openly with God about all matters of life during any moment in time. Prayer provides an opportunity for Covenant believers to express their heartfelt adoration, confessions, thanksgiving and love to God. Prayer allows Christians to seek God's guidance and will for their life. Also, prayer enables ordinary believers to intercede on the behalf of others to God and partner with God in destroying the plans of the enemy. Most of all, prayer is the opportunity for God's people to have honest, open and personal conversations with Him.

Prayer is the act of the saints working together with God via the union of the believer's thoughts with God's will. Prayer is the audible effort of agreement and affirmation of God's will to be accomplished. Subsequently, prayer is not a median of self-serving change. It isn't the activity of bargaining or a tool that can be used to manipulate the ears of God for one's personal gain. Prayer can't alter God's plans; prayer merely archives what God has already established and preordained.

God reserves His power for use in conjunction with the prayers of believers. Within the context of His power, the earth is given governing authority over heaven via the spiritual order of binding and loosing what's achieved through prayer. God will only bind or loose in heaven what His children have first bound and loosed on earth through prayer. "Truly I tell you, whatever you bind on earth will be bound in heaven, and whatever you loose on earth will be loosed in heaven." – Matthew 18:18

And God does not bind and loose in isolation; there is a covenant relationship at work, and He delights in letting us seek His will so the blessing of binding and loosing can happen. God waits for the free will of His people on earth to prayerfully bind and loose before He acts because His methods cause us to become more useful in His hands. We grow deeper in faith when we realize that lining up with God's will can result in a more effective prayer life. As such, we become invested co-laborers with God in prayer. We become God's deputized change agents with spiritual authority to reveal His will and promises. But the power to bind and loose is only available within the salvific relationship and the act of faith. Otherwise, our prayers merely become empty sounds that form words that are void of power and purpose.

Therefore, it is my hope that this book will help you to understand that your prayers are cooperative moments used to fulfill God's will, not to just satisfy your needs, but rather to help you reach a position of recognized purpose and a daily attitude of self-denial. Self-denial is essential to a healthy prayer life because it refuses the desires of the flesh and increases the opportunities for God's will to manifest in and through your life. Too often, people think prayer is a medium used to express the wants and desires of the petitioner. But you should know that God seeks to use you to accomplish His purposes in the earth through your prayers. As such, when you're lined up with the will of God, you're better able to realize that His will can become a real means of fulfilling your need. Thus, you shouldn't pray for selfish needs. In fact, your needs should be united with God and surrendered to His will. It's the act of surrendering that causes the blessings to flow, miracles to manifest, changes to happen, and promises to be revealed.

As Christians, when we consider the practice of praying we should understand that our faith is the foundational binding agent of our prayer life. Jesus Christ is the cornerstone of the Christian faith, but the bricks of our spirituality are set by the mortar of our faith in God. As such, nothing manifests itself in the prayers of a person who doesn't believe that God is capable or willing to act upon their prayerful request. Furthermore, as Christians, we should understand that our prayers are reliant on the health of our relationship with God in respect to the sinfulness that may exist in our lives. We must willfully maintain a lifestyle built on the foundation of Christ, so our prayers to God aren't impeded by the activities of sin or Satan. Thus, our daily prayer life is serious, and the work of prayer is therefore real work tied to real accomplishments. And when we couple our faith, intentions, heart, and self-denial with the will of God in prayer the expectation is a prayer revolution – a real Prayvolution!

# BEGIN YOUR PRAYVOLUTION

Please partner with me as I cover this book in a prayer that's sealed in the name of Christ Jesus.

*Glorious and wonderful God of heaven, please hear my petition. Lord, you know the humble meditations of my heart and the sin that resides in its hidden spaces. You know the accomplishments of my hands and the failings of my flesh. You know the purpose of my life and the stumbles of my journey. And yet, despite all of my faults, all of my failures, all of my struggles, you still love me enough to wake me up each day under the shadow of your right hand. You still set my feet on the promises of eternity with a purpose to become what you have destined for my life. Lord, use everything that I have written in this book to transform lives, to heal souls, to set people free, to inspire hope and greatness, to promote ideas, to encourage forward movement, and to deliver people to the point of a prayer revolution. God let every letter, word, and sentence in this book be used to give confidence, faith, hope, peace, humility, love, compassion and a divine certainty that comes from a strong and mature prayer life. Let this book be a tool for those who have decided to stand on the wall as mighty intercessors for their family, community, church, nation and this world. Use this book to become a starting point of determination to know you better and to have a deeper relationship with you. Lord, start a Prayvolution in the heart of every reader and let your might hand be shown in their lives. I offer this humble prayer in the revolutionary name of Jesus Christ. Amen.*

# PRAYER DAYS 1 – 10

"To be a Christian without prayer is no more possible than to be alive without breathing." – Martin Luther

# DAY 1

## The Need For Thankful Prayer

*Be anxious for nothing, but in everything by prayer and supplication
with thanksgiving let your requests be made known to God;* —
Philippians 4:6 NKJV

Lord of unspeakable joy, there's no one like you, no help, no power, no one greater than you. When you birthed me into this world, you breathed life into my body connecting me to you. When I accepted Jesus Christ as my Lord and Savior, your Holy Spirit came to live in my body making the essence of your breath come alive in me and filling me with the power of your flame. Today, I ask for your forgiveness. Forgive me for not nourishing the Holy flame within me, for not reading your Holy Word faithfully, for not communing with your people daily, for not making my body a living sacrifice of holiness. Use me today Lord and teach me how to access the fire within. Lord, teach me how to be ready in the presence of my enemies, negativity, trials, and hardships. Help me to be ready to glorify you at all times so that the world may see a portion of your Spirit in action. Use me to help the lost, the weak, and those who are seeking to know that you're the one true Living God. It's in the powerful name of Jesus Christ that I pray. Amen.

## Personal Questions and Prayer Journal - Date:

What key words stuck out to you in this prayer? List three or four of those words.

How did you feel after reading this prayer? List two or three of your feelings.

Now write your own intimate prayer to God and think about the words you wrote down and your feelings. Tell God what's on your heart and mind. Remember, He's listening, and He wants to hear from you.

# DAY 2

## Manifestations Of God's Power

*I pray that the eyes of your heart may be enlightened in order that you may know the hope to which he has called you, the riches of his glorious inheritance in his holy people, and his incomparably great power for us who believe. That power is the same as the mighty strength.* — Ephesians 1:18-19

God of the right now and on time, your power is unimaginable and unattainable. Yet, Lord, you're gentle and graceful in the most tender and fragile areas of my life. You O' God have the ability to create and destroy the gifts of life with the power of a single word. You have the power to raise majestic mountains and carve out valleys for the oceans. You have the power to suspend the sparkling constellations and rotate the celestial galaxies. Still, in all of those great moments of wondrous power, you took the time to breathe your breath of being into my unworthy lungs this morning. In all of your greatness Lord, you found something in me today that was beyond man's comprehension and worth redeeming, so I thank you. Father, you're truly awesome beyond words or imagination, and I'm glad that you're my God. So today God, I want to worship you for being God of the universe, God of the heavens, and God of my life. And Lord, I want you to know that I love you beyond the understating of my limited words. It's in the mighty and saving name of Jesus the Christ that I pray. Amen.

## Personal Questions and Prayer Journal - Date:

What key words stuck out to you in this prayer? List three or four of those words.

How did you feel after reading this prayer? List two or three of your feelings.

Now write your own intimate prayer to God and think about the words you wrote down and your feelings. Tell God what's on your heart and mind. Remember, He's listening, and He wants to hear from you.

# DAY 3

## Keeping Your Focus On God

*You will keep in perfect peace*
*those whose minds are steadfast,*
*because they trust in you.* — Isaiah 26:3

Sovereign God of power and peace, my thoughts aren't your thoughts, and my ways aren't your ways. But my spirit should be pursuing the call of your thoughts, and the actions of my life should be an example of your ways. Unfortunately, God, I haven't always heard your thoughts or lived out your ways for my life, so I'm humbly and submissively seeking your forgiveness today. Lord, I need a fresh drenching of your Spirit to rain down over me, so that I can be washed clean of the things that aren't like you. I want to be renewed by the breath of your Spirit so that I can become all that you have created me to be. Lord, I need you to take hold of me today, scrape off the residue of sin and polish me up again so that my cup can be filled to an overflowing with the fullness of your being. God, I need my mind and heart to be cleared of the trappings of this world so that I can focus on you, hear you, walk with you and talk with you like never before. God rescue me today from my malnourished state of spirituality and fill me with the supernatural bread of your life so that I'll be able to serve you completely. Father, I ask these things to be heard and accepted in the name of my Lord and Savior Jesus the Christ. Amen.

## Personal Questions and Prayer Journal - Date:

What key words stuck out to you in this prayer? List three or four of those words.

How did you feel after reading this prayer? List two or three of your feelings.

Now write your own intimate prayer to God and think about the words you wrote down and your feelings. Tell God what's on your heart and mind. Remember, He's listening, and He wants to hear from you.

# DAY 4

## There Is Freedom In The Truth

*Then you will know the truth, and the truth will set you free.* — John 8:32

God of liberation and justice, I thank you for the truth of your Holy Word and the freedom that I have gained because of it. I thank you for sending the truth into my life, the true meaning of your love in the form of my Lord and Savior Jesus. But let me go one step further, God, in proclaiming my gratitude about the truth. Lord, I'm also grateful for the truth of my past. I'm blessed because the truth of my past has helped to shape me into the person that I am today. I'm grateful for the good and the bad because you used these truths to guide me closer to you. Father, you used the truth of my life like a winnowing fork until the "Spirit of Truth" was the only thing left between you and me. It was the truth of your promise in my life that enabled me to become accepting of your Holy Word. It was the truth of your love that drew me near to your heart and allowed me to embrace salvation freely. Lord, it was the truth of your grace that transformed me into a better person, and it was the truth of your mercy that washed the true sins of my life away. Lord, thank you for your wonderful truth because it allows me to proclaim the power of your transforming Word in the presence of those who would seek to use the truth of my past against me. God, I thank you for the entire truth, since it was the whole truth that truly set me free. It's in Jesus' name that I pray. Amen.

## Personal Questions and Prayer Journal - Date:

What key words stuck out to you in this prayer? List three or four of those words.

How did you feel after reading this prayer? List two or three of your feelings.

Now write your own intimate prayer to God and think about the words you wrote down and your feelings. Tell God what's on your heart and mind. Remember, He's listening, and He wants to hear from you.

# DAY 5

## There Is An Inheritance With Your Name On It

*"to be put into effect when the times reach their fulfillment – to bring unity to all things in heaven and on earth under Christ.*

*In him we were also chosen, having been predestined according to the plan of him who works out everything in conformity with the purpose of his will,"* — Ephesians 1:10-11

God of faithful promises, the world says that I'm nothing without material riches, but that isn't true. You have made me more than rich. You have made me eternally wealthy and I'm grateful for this fact. God, I thank you for extending the covenant of salvation, joy, peace, relationship and hope to someone like me. I thank you for setting a place for me at your banquet table of eternal blessings. God, I thank you for loving me so much that you sent your Son to die on a criminal's cross of shame so that I might live a life of undeserved grace. And because of Jesus' death, the chokehold of sin was destroyed in my life. And because of Jesus' resurrection, I have inherited His amazing love and eternal life. You O' Lord have made me an heir to a guaranteed inheritance in Christ that the world cannot understand or measure. The world cannot fathom the love that I have for you or the joy that resides in my heart. So Lord, never let me forget the price you paid for me and never let me forget that unmerited grace that you afford me every day. It's in the name of my Lord and Savior Jesus the Christ that I pray. Amen.

## Personal Questions and Prayer Journal - Date:

What key words stuck out to you in this prayer? List three or four of those words.

How did you feel after reading this prayer? List two or three of your feelings.

Now write your own intimate prayer to God and think about the words you wrote down and your feelings. Tell God what's on your heart and mind. Remember, He's listening, and He wants to hear from you.

# DAY 6

## Claiming Your Position

*For he chose us in him before the creation of the world to be holy and blameless in his sight.* — Ephesians 1:4

Mighty God, great King, and awesome Ruler, I thank you for your meticulousness and thoughtfulness in creating me. Thank you for designing me to be a wonderfully unique person. There's no other soul on this earth that is like me; therefore, no one can accomplish the task that you have set aside for me to complete. That's why I want to be more devoted to living out your plan for my life so that your hand can be glorified in the earth. Lord, forgive me for not living up to the fullness of the calling on my life and for not taking serious the position that you have created me to hold. God, lift me up today so that I can escape the mindset that has limited and prevented me from yielding to the total commitment that is required so that I can live out a true sacrificial life. Father, I love you, and without you, I can do nothing, so I commit myself to the purpose of your design and you, right now. It's in the mighty name of my risen Lord and Savior Jesus the Christ that I pray. Amen.

## Personal Questions and Prayer Journal - Date:

What key words stuck out to you in this prayer? List three or four of those words.

How did you feel after reading this prayer? List two or three of your feelings.

Now write your own intimate prayer to God and think about the words you wrote down and your feelings. Tell God what's on your heart and mind. Remember, He's listening, and He wants to hear from you.

# DAY 7

## Got To Have His Grace, Peace, Mercy

*To Timothy my true son in the faith:*
*Grace, mercy and peace from God the Father and Christ Jesus our*
*Lord.* — 1Timothy 1:2

Lord, I shabach your name. I praise you for being my God and seeing me through eyes of grace, peace, and mercy. Though I don't deserve to take another breath, you O' Lord have seen something in me that's worthy of your eternal Love. So, thank you, God, for allowing me to live. Father, where would I be if not for your grace? What would I do if your mercy had a limited human perspective? How could I make it if your peace did not well up inside me and overflow in times of sorrow, confusion, and trouble? You're God, and I thank you for seeing beyond my present horizon. Lord, thank you for carrying me on the wings of your character. Lord, thank you for allowing me to see another day, another opportunity to get it right. Now Lord, help me to become a beacon of your grace, peace, and mercy in the home, workplace, school, and community. Help me to become a testimony so that I can be used to draw people closer to you so that they can experience fully who God is. Lord, I surrender to you today. I pray and ask all these things in the name of my Lord and Savior Jesus. Amen.

## Personal Questions and Prayer Journal - Date:

What key words stuck out to you in this prayer? List three or four of those words.

How did you feel after reading this prayer? List two or three of your feelings.

Now write your own intimate prayer to God and think about the words you wrote down and your feelings. Tell God what's on your heart and mind. Remember, He's listening, and He wants to hear from you.

# DAY 8

## I Will Rejoice On Both Sides

*Though the fig tree does not bud*
  *and there are no grapes on the vines,*
*though the olive crop fails*
  *and the fields produce no food,*
*though there are no sheep in the pen*
  *and no cattle in the stalls,*
*yet I will rejoice in the Lord,*
  *I will be joyful in God my Savior.* — Habakkuk 3:17-18

Most merciful God, help me to endure the issues of right now. I want to give you the glory by testifying to the world that it was you who carried me to the other side. Lord, hear my plea and answer it with a mighty wind of change because the earth is crying out to you through the blood of wars, the rainless droughts of depression, the senseless famines of injustice and the raging fires of immortally. God, the land is crying out to you because the people have closed up their hearts and mouths, so now the rocks are crying out. But the rocks don't have dominion over this earth; we do. So, forgive us today God for not taking our rightful place in the sanctuary of your courts and praising you through these painful times. Forgive us, God, for not standing on the promise that you would never leave us nor forsake us. Forgive us for only praising you in the good times and not praising you with more vigor in the not so good times. Forgive us for not being more reckless and undignified in our reverence for might works and love. As such Lord, I'm asking in prayer that you shower down your presence by letting the gates of your blessed waters rain over these United States, so that the drought can be overcome and the fires can be cast down. In addition, God, let the gifts of your Holy presence fill and saturate the hearts of the people so that we can be drawn closer to you and end the raging internal and external wars. Father, heal this land and its people from the inside out and let us never forget to praise you even when we make it through to the other side.

## Personal Questions and Prayer Journal - Date:

What key words stuck out to you in this prayer? List three or four of those words.

How did you feel after reading this prayer? List two or three of your feelings.

Now write your own intimate prayer to God and think about the words you wrote down and your feelings. Tell God what's on your heart and mind. Remember, He's listening, and He wants to hear from you.

# DAY 9

## Moving Forward By His Grace

*You see, at just the right time, when we were still powerless, Christ died for the ungodly.*

*But God demonstrates his own love for us in this: While we were still sinners, Christ died for us.* — Romans 5:6,8

Loving Creator, my El, my Father, I thank you for your ever-present merciful kindness that you have shown during my times of sinning. I praise you for helping me overcome the areas of my life that have hindered the shaping my life for your divine hands. God, today I ask that you reach down and touch the spaces in my life that aren't like Jesus and transform them so that They're pleasing and acceptable in your sight. Touch me today Lord and guide me as I do my best to walk with you. Father, wash the unclean places in my life, take away the unhealthy habits that block my spiritual connection to you and bind up the relationships that have held me back from going higher in life. Lord God, set me free from the bondage of my past and the chains of my present and destroy that plans of the enemy concerning my life. I love you, God and I need you today, right now. It's in the name of Jesus the Christ that I pray. Amen.

## Personal Questions and Prayer Journal - Date:

What key words stuck out to you in this prayer? List three or four of those words.

How did you feel after reading this prayer? List two or three of your feelings.

Now write your own intimate prayer to God and think about the words you wrote down and your feelings. Tell God what's on your heart and mind. Remember, He's listening, and He wants to hear from you.

# DAY 10

## The Key To Prosperity

*In everything that he undertook in the service of God's temple and in obedience to the law and the commands, he sought his God and worked wholeheartedly. And so he prospered.* — 2 Chronicles 31:21

God, transform me from the inside out so that I may glorify your name at home, at work, around friends, and family. Father God, I want you to line up my spirit with yours so that I can know how to work out and work through troubling situations. Help me to remain committed to my faith and obedient to your commands so that I can prosper. Help me to remain committed to reading your word so that I can prosper. Help me to remain committed to loving my family so that I can prosper. Help me to remain committed to loving my neighbor so that I can prosper. Lord, help me to remain committed to living out my purpose in life so that I can prosper. It's in Jesus' name that I pray. Amen.

## Personal Questions and Prayer Journal - Date:

What key words stuck out to you in this prayer? List three or four of those words.

How did you feel after reading this prayer? List two or three of your feelings.

Now write your own intimate prayer to God and think about the words you wrote down and your feelings. Tell God what's on your heart and mind. Remember, He's listening, and He wants to hear from you.

# PRAYER DAYS 11 – 20

"Your very being as a Christian depends upon your still clinging, still trusting, still depending. This He must give you, for it all comes from Him and Him alone. To sum it all up, if you want that splendid power in prayer, you must remain in loving, living, lasting, conscious, practical, abiding union with the Lord Jesus Christ," – C. H. Spurgeon

# DAY 11

## A Great Deposit Of His Joy

*I have told you this so that my joy may be in you and that your joy may be complete.* — John 15:11

Awesome God, wonderful God, and mighty God. I bless your Holy name. I'm thankful for the love that you have continued to pour over my life. Even though, I fall short and have allowed sin to influence me on more occasions, your beckoning love for me has never wavered or diminished. God, I thank you for being my Lord, because when I think about the events of my life, I'm made joyful in knowing that it was your love that has carried me through every troubled moment. Your sacrificial love has provided me freedom from the evils of this word. Your sacrificial love has also provided me with the fullness of your Joy that flows from Emanuel's veins. Consequently, Lord, the blood of redemption that flowed over me at Calvary and the Holy Spirit that is alive within me has compounded your supernatural Joy in my life. That is why I can praise and worship you with the fullness of my heart. Please don't ever take your Joy from me. Make the supply of your joy available today, tomorrow, and all the days after. It's in the name of Jesus the Christ that I pray. Amen.

## Personal Questions and Prayer Journal - Date:

What key words stuck out to you in this prayer? List three or four of those words.

What are some of your favorite Christian or Gospel songs? Think about the lyrics.

Now write your own prayer using the words you wrote down and the song lyrics. Tell God what's on your heart and mind. He's listening for your heart.

# DAY 12

## There Is Strength In Your Meekness

*Blessed are the meek,*
*for they will inherit the earth* — Matthew 5:5

Gracious God, I glorify you for reconciling me unto yourself and covering me with the garment of your mercy. Lord, It's in your awesome presence that I have found peace, love and purpose. It's in your presence that I have found the true strength of humility. It's in your hands that I can find the kind of strength that is encompassed in the act of submitting myself to your divine will, a strength that is displayed by the characteristic of meekness. That is why I submit myself to you daily so that I can become the spiritual person that you have purposed me to be. Open my heart Jesus and fill me with the powerful quietness of your humility. Use me and send me out to be a blessing to those that are seeking and need your peace. It's in the awesome name of Jesus the Christ that I pray. Amen.

## Personal Questions and Prayer Journal - Date:

What key words stuck out to you in this prayer? List three or four of those words.

What are some of your favorite Christian or Gospel songs? Think about the lyrics.

Now write your own prayer using the words you wrote down and the song lyrics. Tell God what's on your heart and mind. He's listening for your heart.

# DAY 13

## The Power Of Integrity

*Because of my integrity you uphold me
and set me in your presence forever.* — Psalms 41:12

Jehovah-Tsidkenu "The Lord our Righteousness," I thank you for being Truth and speaking the truth into my life in the face of opposition, blame, gossip, and wickedness. In addition, God, I praise you for guiding me along that path of integrity and for providing me with the spiritual boundaries of conviction when I stray. Because of your integrity Lord, I'm able of overcome my past mistakes, endure my present trials, and I have been made ready for the challenges of my future; for that I'm grateful. Let the aroma of your integrity continue to be a daily fragrant reminder for my actions and intentions. It's in Jesus' name that I pray. Amen.

## Personal Questions and Prayer Journal - Date:

What key words stuck out to you in this prayer? List three or four of those words.

What are some of your favorite Christian or Gospel songs? Think about the lyrics.

Now write your own prayer using the words you wrote down and the song lyrics. Tell God what's on your heart and mind. He's listening for your heart.

# DAY 14

## Bring His Peace With You

*Settle matters quickly with your adversary . . .* — Matthew 5:25
NKJV

Lord of justice and peace, please continue to instruct me in the ways of your truth and wisdom so that I may grow as an anointed child of your eternal vine and become more Christ-like in my heart, soul, mind, and spirit. Show me how to bring the presence of your peace into every kind of conflict. Help me to share the compassion, forgiveness, humility, love, and kindness that you have deposited within me. Lead me in showing the world that your grace and mercy is available to everyone in every situation. Help me to become a present messenger of love and a witness of your perfect will. It's in the mighty and matchless name of Jesus the Christ that I pray. Amen.

## Personal Questions and Prayer Journal - Date:

What key words stuck out to you in this prayer? List three or four of those words.

What are some of your favorite Christian or Gospel songs? Think about the lyrics.

Now write your own prayer using the words you wrote down and the song lyrics. Tell God what's on your heart and mind. He's listening for your heart.

# DAY 15

## Press On Beyond Your Past

*Brothers and sisters, I do not consider myself yet to have taken hold of it. But one thing I do: Forgetting what is behind and straining toward what's ahead,* — Philippians 3:13

Lord of the Turn-Around! I know that I cannot fully comprehend the depths of your mind, heart or love. But what I do know is that I'm special enough that you chose to wake me up this morning, and this fact qualifies me beyond what the world can see. God, I'm thankful for the blood that you allowed to be shed on the cross. Thank you for the unselfish sin destroying sacrifice by my Savior Jesus Christ. That selfless and painful act came at a price that I can never repay. And it motivates me to press on towards becoming all that you have created me to be. So, today, I'm taking off the chains of my past. I'm breaking the shackles that have kept me from fully experiencing a deeper relationship with you. And I'm going to be intentional about understanding my purpose on this earth and in the lives if your people. Father, let the past remain in the ashes and let the dust of my life be formed in your hand. Use me Lord so that the world can know that you have a plan and a purpose for everyone. In the name of Jesus Christ, I pray. Amen.

## Personal Questions and Prayer Journal - Date:

What key words stuck out to you in this prayer? List three or four of those words.

What are some of your favorite Christian or Gospel songs? Think about the lyrics.

Now write your own prayer using the words you wrote down and the song lyrics. Tell God what's on your heart and mind. He's listening for your heart.

# DAY 16

## Chasing After The Grace Of God

*As God's co-workers we urge you not to receive God's grace in vain.*
— 2 Corinthians 6:1

Glorious and Magnificent Father, I need, and I'm thankful for your unmerited grace that flows over my life today. Despite my inconsistent actions and reactions to the struggles of life, your love has and does remain constant, and for that I'm grateful. Lord, your mercy has spared me and carried me over the obstacles of my own creation, and for that I'm humbled. So, God, help me to grow higher, wider, and deeper in the love that you poured down over me so that the world can see your love in action as I walk in the grace that you provide. Help me to recognize the power of your delivering hand so that I can share the truth of your grace with the person that needs to hear about it today. And I'll be careful to give you all of the honor and the praise in the name of Jesus the Christ. Amen.

## Personal Questions and Prayer Journal - Date:

What key words stuck out to you in this prayer? List three or four of those words.

What are some of your favorite Christian or Gospel songs? Think about the lyrics.

Now write your own prayer using the words you wrote down and the song lyrics. Tell God what's on your heart and mind. He's listening for your heart.

# DAY 17

## Asking Jesus To Speak To You

*In the past God spoke to our ancestors through the prophets at many times and in various ways, but in these last days he has spoken to us by his Son...* — Hebrews 1:1-2a

Heavenly Father, my God, and King, I need to hear your voice. I need to know that you're with me. I want to walk with you and to talk with you today. I want to remove every obstacle that impedes the spiritual connection that you have made available to me. Lord, remove anything in my path that is hindering me from hearing or seeing your attempts to communicate with me. God, take the blinds off of my spiritual eyes and orientate my carnal mind to the proper direction of your truth so that I can recognize the instructions that you're giving and the path that you have laid before me. Father, let your will be my comfort and guide forever in times of trouble and need. Speak to me Jesus and let your presence be powerfully known. It's in Jesus' name that I pray. Amen.

## Personal Questions and Prayer Journal - Date:

What key words stuck out to you in this prayer? List three or four of those words.

What are some of your favorite Christian or Gospel songs? Think about the lyrics.

Now write your own prayer using the words you wrote down and the song lyrics. Tell God what's on your heart and mind. He's listening for your heart.

# DAY 18

## Let God Work Out His Power In You

*Therefore, my dear friends, as you have always obeyed – not only in my presence, but now much more in my absence – continue to work out your salvation with fear and trembling, for it is God who works in you to will and to act in order to fulfill his good purpose.* — Philippians 2:12-13

Awesome and Glorious God, open my heart and purify my mind so that your will can fall fresh over me today. Give me the strength and the courage to stand on the truth of your will and every Holy Word that is made alive in me. Shape my spiritual hearing and eyes so that your voice and movements can be made clear to my soul. God, let your will continually be my one true source at all times. Push me to the mark of greatness in your name. Force me to always be mindful of your presence. And set your fire down in my soul so that I can burn with the purpose of sharing your love for all. It's the mighty and matchless name of Christ Jesus that I pray. Amen.

## Personal Questions and Prayer Journal - Date:

What key words stuck out to you in this prayer? List three or four of those words.

What are some of your favorite Christian or Gospel songs? Think about the lyrics.

Now write your own prayer using the words you wrote down and the song lyrics. Tell God what's on your heart and mind. He's listening for your heart.

# DAY 19

## Changing Your Carnal Mind

*You are still worldly. For since there is jealousy and quarreling among you, are you not worldly? ...* — 1 Corinthians 3:3

Eternal Father, God of all that I am and all that I'll ever be, I give you praise. Lord, touch me today in the spaces of my heart that aren't pleasing and acceptable to you. Show me the things that I need to give up in this world. Show me the things that I need to confess and give me the strength to overcome the temptations of this life. Renew my spirit daily so that I may bring glory, honor, and magnification to your name. Use me in the acts of your will so that your Kingdom can be advanced in this earth. Push down and shake together every skill, talent, and gift so that I can be used to help lift your name higher though the actions of my walk. It's in the name of my Lord and Savior Jesus Christ that I pray. Amen.

## Personal Questions and Prayer Journal - Date:

What key words stuck out to you in this prayer? List three or four of those words.

What are some of your favorite Christian or Gospel songs? Think about the lyrics.

Now write your own prayer using the words you wrote down and the song lyrics. Tell God what's on your heart and mind. He's listening for your heart.

# DAY 20

## Resurrect Your Amazing Faith

This Prayer is for many of us that have experienced something in our lives that seemed impossible. Yet, we were able to complete the task, overcome the odds, reach the goal, accomplish the vision, etc. Somehow, the power to move that figurative or literal mountain welled up within us, and for a moment or longer, we felt that unexplainable power that has been deposited within us by the Holy Spirit. Basically, we felt God, and we came to life like never before. Well, I'm here to say that we can deposit that same power back into or past dreams. We can pour back into those same dreams that once seemed to send a fire through our bones because they don't have to remain dead any longer. It's a fact that the awesome power we have felt on occasion is still within us today. We must remember that we can do all things that seem impossible once we align ourselves with the will of God. So, take the initiative today and go back and get your dreams, dig them up and pour the power of prayer and God back into them. Amen!

> *This is why it is said:*
> *"Wake up, sleeper,*
> *rise from the dead,*
> *and Christ will shine on you."* — Ephesians 5:14

Great and Mighty God, help me to harness the awesome power that you have deposited within me. Help me to focus and unleash my faith so that I can take authority over all things that you have placed in my past, present, and future. Help me to resurrect those dreams that are aligned with your will so that I can bring glory to your name and help to usher in your Kingdom to this earthly realm. It's in the awesome name of Jesus Christ that I pray. Amen!

## Personal Questions and Prayer Journal - Date:

What key words stuck out to you in this prayer? List three or four of those words.

What are some of your favorite Christian or Gospel songs? Think about the lyrics.

Now write your own prayer using the words you wrote down and the song lyrics. Tell God what's on your heart and mind. He's listening for your heart.

# PRAYER DAYS 21 – 30

"Prayer is the nearest approach to God and the
highest enjoyment of Him that we are capable
of in this life. It is the noblest exercise of the
soul, the most exalted use of our best faculties,
the highest imitation of the blessed inhabitants
of heaven." – William Law

# DAY 21

## You Will Not Be Worried

*Do not be anxious about anything, but in every situation, by prayer and petition, with thanksgiving, present your requests to God. And the peace of God, which transcends all understanding, will guard your hearts and your minds in Christ Jesus.* — Philippians 4:6-7

God of Boldness and Truth, help me to overcome my times of worry by supplying me with a portion of your peace. Rain down over me, Lord, and saturate my mind so that I may glorify your name in the midst of my troubles. Father, you're *Jehovah-Shalom* (the Lord our Peace), therefore in your presence I'm safe, and your peace is my rock. Now, Father let your peace be manifested in my actions so that the Spirit of Christ may be witnessed in my life. It's in Jesus' name that I pray. Amen.

## Personal Questions and Prayer Journal - Date:

What key words stuck out to you in this prayer? List three or four of those words.

What are some of your favorite bible verses? Write down one or two verses.

Now write your own prayer using the words you wrote down and the bible verses. Talk to God about what's going around you by lifting your words to his ears. He's wants to hear from His child.

# DAY 22

## You Can Be Rooted Deep In Jesus

*Blessed is the one*
*who does not walk in step with the wicked*
*or stand in the way that sinners take*
*or sit in the company of mockers,*
*but whose delight is in the law of the Lord,*
*and who meditates on his law day and night.*
*That person is like a tree planted by streams of water,*
*which yields its fruit in season*
*and whose leaf does not wither –*
*whatever they do prospers.* — Psalm 1:1-3

Lord of the deep, let your perfect will fall fresh on me today so that I might go out into this dark world and share your magnificent light. Lord, help me to share your Kingdom with the lost, confused, broken, "unchurched," and unbelieving and desperate people of this world. Enable me to stand firm knowing that you're the Truth and the Way. And without you, I can do nothing. But through you, I can do all things. Let your will be my will and let your love be my love so that I can share them with those whom you have placed in my path. It's in the mighty name of Jesus Christ that I pray. Amen!

## Personal Questions and Prayer Journal - Date:

What key words stuck out to you in this prayer? List three or four of those words.

What are some of your favorite bible verses? Write down one or two verses.

Now write your own prayer using the words you wrote down and the bible verses. Talk to God about what's going around you by lifting your words to his ears. He's wants to hear from His child.

# DAY 23

## God Is Working His Word In You

*For the word of God is alive and active. Sharper than any double – edged sword, it penetrates even to dividing soul and spirit, joints and marrow; it judges the thoughts and attitudes of the heart.* — Hebrews 4:12

God, search my heart today and cleanse my soul. Send the Holy Spirit to scrub my thoughts with your truths about my life. Allow this my flesh to die daily so that the spiritual witness within me can testify about Word and your will. Lord, let the power of your word penetrate my heart, let it circulate within my blood until it becomes a sweet aroma to everyone that I encounter. Let your scriptures rest on my lips so that I can be used to bring comfort to the wounded and healing to the broken. Father turn every negative into a testimony about your actions in my life. Use all of me today until I'm poured out and empty. It's in Jesus' name that I pray. Amen.

## Personal Questions and Prayer Journal - Date:

What key words stuck out to you in this prayer? List three or four of those words.

What are some of your favorite bible verses? Write down one or two verses.

Now write your own prayer using the words you wrote down and the bible verses. Talk to God about what's going around you by lifting your words to his ears. He's wants to hear from His child.

# DAY 24

## Chasing The Abundant Life

*Now to him who is able to do immeasurably more than all we ask or imagine, according to his power that is at work within us, —*
Ephesians 3:20

Lord of Amazing Miracles, thank you for your provision of unmerited favor and blessings. Thank you for the multiple talents that you have given me because they have allowed me to accomplish my personal goals. Father, I'm asking for your forgiveness today because I know that I have not always used these gifts to glorify your name or your will for my life. Have mercy on me today, God, for letting my own limited understanding dictate my faith and actions. Lord, help me to see beyond my own horizon so that I can do the work that you have predestined me to fulfill. Use me so that I can hear that you're well pleased with my life. Father, help me to become a better steward and servant today, tomorrow and thereafter. It's in Jesus' name that I pray. Amen.

## Personal Questions and Prayer Journal - Date:

What key words stuck out to you in this prayer? List three or four of those words.

What are some of your favorite bible verses? Write down one or two verses.

Now write your own prayer using the words you wrote down and the bible verses. Talk to God about what's going around you by lifting your words to his ears. He's wants to hear from His child.

# DAY 25

## Winning The Great Race

*I have fought the good fight, I have finished the race, I have kept the faith.* — 2 Timothy 4:7

Lord of the Next Mile, thank you for allowing me to see this new day and for allowing me to enter in this great race you have called me to participate in. Lord, give me the spirit of David and the perseverance of Paul so that I'll have the courage and the determination to continue forward in the face of all obstacles and troubles. But most of all, God, give me the boldness of Jesus so that I'll have the faith to move in any direction that you have asked me to go. The faith to stand strong in the presence of my enemies. The faith to be a light in the presence of darkness. The faith to carry my cross daily. And the faith to love a world that doesn't love you or me. It's in Blood brought faith of Jesus Christ that I pray. Amen.

## Personal Questions and Prayer Journal - Date:

What key words stuck out to you in this prayer? List three or four of those words.

What are some of your favorite bible verses? Write down one or two verses.

Now write your own prayer using the words you wrote down and the bible verses. Talk to God about what's going around you by lifting your words to his ears. He's wants to hear from His child.

# DAY 26

## Asking God To Shape Your Life

*His divine power has given us everything we need for a godly life through our knowledge of him who called us by his own glory and goodness.* — 2 Peter 1:3

Dear Master Potter, please help me today. Lord, restore the broken pieces of my life and give me a miracle to fit my need. I praise you right now, Father, through all of the unhappy circumstances in my life. And I'm holding on to the deposits of joy, peace, mercy and grace that you have so lovingly granted me every day. Lord, change the areas of my life that aren't pleasing to you and grant me the favor in your Kingdom and on this earth. God, thank you for continued shaping and renewing of my life. Thank you for steadying my feet and helping me to stand on the Rock of you Word. It's in Jesus' name that I plead this prayer at the foot of your throne. Amen.

## Personal Questions and Prayer Journal - Date:

What key words stuck out to you in this prayer? List three or four of those words.

What are some of your favorite bible verses? Write down one or two verses.

Now write your own prayer using the words you wrote down and the bible verses. Talk to God about what's going around you by lifting your words to his ears. He's wants to hear from His child.

# DAY 27

## Standing Against Temptations

*The tempter came to him and said, "If you are the Son of God, tell these stones to become bread." —* Matthew 4:3

Father of protection and provision, press down into my mind and spirit the discernment, faith, wisdom, and strength that is required to defeat the Devil and to accomplish your will for my life. Lord, open my ears, eyes, and heart today so that I can hear you more clearly and see the path that you have called me to walk. Let the meditations of my mind and heart be found pleasing and acceptable to you. Let the words of my mouth speak life, and the reflection of my face be shown in the image of your character. Let my feet stand with strength and power against the plans of every kind of enemy. It's in the covering name of Jesus that I pray. Amen.

## Personal Questions and Prayer Journal - Date:

What key words stuck out to you in this prayer? List three or four of those words.

What are some of your favorite bible verses? Write down one or two verses.

Now write your own prayer using the words you wrote down and the bible verses. Talk to God about what's going around you by lifting your words to his ears. He's wants to hear from His child.

# DAY 28

## Cultivating A Heart That Loves God

*For I desire mercy, not sacrifice, and acknowledgment of God rather than burnt offerings.* — Hosea 6:6

Heavenly Father and Lord of my life, I give you thanks today for loving me in a manner that goes beyond my understanding. I thank you God for not seeing me through the eyes of humanity. I'm grateful that you are my omnipotent deliverer because your love for me is greater than the love I have for myself. And you have saved me from many things in this world, including myself. So, I'm humbly asking that you pour out a portion of your boldness in love over my life and spirit so that I may be lead from the inside out. Cleanse me today, Lord, and shower down an affectionate anointing that binds me closer to you so that I can serve you better. Write on the scroll of my heart today and pen your purpose for my life. Send the Holy Spirit to show me the right way to go. I ask that these things be done in the name of Jesus the Christ. Amen!

## Personal Questions and Prayer Journal - Date:

What key words stuck out to you in this prayer? List three or four of those words.

What are some of your favorite bible verses? Write down one or two verses.

Now write your own prayer using the words you wrote down and the bible verses. Talk to God about what's going around you by lifting your words to his ears. He's wants to hear from His child.

# DAY 29

## Breaking The Chain Of Anger

*"In your anger do not sin": Do not let the sun go down while you are still angry,* — Ephesians 4:26

Lord of the Calm and Stillness, come into my heart right now and purge the residue of my past that has kept me from being at peace. Lord, wash me from the inside out and shower over me from the top of my head to the soles of me feet. Cleanse me of all the things that aren't of you and allow me to walk an upright path so that I may represent all that you have called me to be. God, be with me in my moments of weakness and provide me with the Spirit of Discernment so that I may know the right way to deal with all matters that involve my heart. Touch my mind and break the chain of anger. Crush every link to ashes. Heal every space in my heart and memory that has been bruised by the arrows of life. Show me how to live happy, joy-filled and stress-free. Place the words of your peaceful miracles on my lips and in my heart so that I can share the hope of freedom today. Now let my prayer be heard in the heavens and be received in the name of Jesus Christ. Amen!

## Personal Questions and Prayer Journal - Date:

What key words stuck out to you in this prayer? List three or four of those words.

What are some of your favorite bible verses? Write down one or two verses.

Now write your own prayer using the words you wrote down and the bible verses. Talk to God about what's going around you by lifting your words to his ears. He's wants to hear from His child.

# DAY 30

## Let No One Look Down On You

*Don't let anyone look down on you because you are young, but set an example for the believers in speech, in conduct, in love, in faith and in purity.* — 1 Timothy 4:12

God of the On Time and Right Now, I know that you believe in me. But sometimes I need extra help as I walk the path that your hand has marked out for me. Sometimes I fall short of understanding how great I can be. In the past, I let the negative opinions of others rest on my shoulders. But today is a new day in Christ Jesus. And I feel a breakthrough coming. I can feel my spirit rising up and my mind shaking free of every doubt. I feel the power of your spiritual hands pushing me forward. And as I continue to pray, I feel my faith growing beyond the limits of every negative word spoken over my life. Lord, I declare that I'll be free. I declare that I'll live in great faith. And I declare in the name of Jesus that I'll never look down on my gifts or purpose again. Amen.

## Personal Questions and Prayer Journal - Date:

What key words stuck out to you in this prayer? List three or four of those words.

What are some of your favorite bible verses? Write down one or two verses.

Now write your own prayer using the words you wrote down and the bible verses. Talk to God about what's going around you by lifting your words to his ears. He's wants to hear from His child.

# PRAYER DAYS 31 – 40

"Prayer is the rope that pulls God and man together. But, it doesn't pull God down to us: It pulls us up to Him." – Billy Graham

# DAY 31

## Don't Avoid The Impossible

*Jesus replied, "They do not need to go away. You give them something to eat."* — Matthew 14:16

Amazing Way Maker, help me to embrace the burden of the cross so that I can understand the kind of unapologetic faith that you desire for me possess. Lord, show me how to transcend the image of selfishness that the world is used to seeing. Impart in me a message of love and truth that can help transform the atmosphere on my job, at home, and in my community. Help me to embrace the impossible so that people will know that you're the only miracle maker. Allow me to be a witness to those that need to hear about your love and your on-time provision. And use me to be a comfort to those that need a touch from you. Place the service of your word in my mouth so that others can dine at the table of your truths. It's in the everlasting and all providing name of Jesus that I pray. Amen.

## Personal Questions and Prayer Journal - Date:

What key words stuck out to you in this prayer? List three or four of those words.

List three personal things or feelings (good or not so good) that are on your heart?

Now write your own prayer using the words you wrote down and the heartfelt matters. Tell the Lord about your joy, concern, or sorrows. Let your words be known. God is listening and seeking to meet you.

# DAY 32

## You Can Be Counted Faithful

*I thank Christ Jesus our Lord, who has given me strength, that he considered me trustworthy, appointing me to his service.* — 1 Timothy 1:12

God of revelation and elevation, I thank you for trusting me with the current and undiscovered gifts of my life. Father, today I want to acknowledge that all that I have accomplished and achieved in this life has been made possible by you. But I know that you're not done with my life because I still have more gift and dreams to share with the world. So, Lord, teach me how to be a better servant and a better steward of the gifts that you have freely bestowed upon me. Use me as you see fit. Take from me all that I have to offer and then take some more. And I'll be sure to give you the glory in all things. It's in my Savior's name, Jesus the Christ, that I pray. Amen.

## Personal Questions and Prayer Journal - Date:

What key words stuck out to you in this prayer? List three or four of those words.

List three personal things or feelings (good or not so good) that are on your heart?

Now write your own prayer using the words you wrote down and the heartfelt matters. Tell the Lord about your joy, concern, or sorrows. Let your words be known. God is listening and seeking to meet you.

# DAY 33

## Being The Image Of Grace, Mercy, And Peace

Today's prayer focuses on how Jesus makes the gifts of grace, mercy, and peace available to His children. In addition, to understanding how He supplies these gifts, you should reflect on how you have been formed in His image and likeness. Think about the same loving characteristics of Jesus and see if your life is reflective of His image.

If a change is needed, then today is the perfect opportunity for you to become more like Jesus. Today is an opportunity to mend broken relationships, heal friendships or supply some cash to a person in need. Today is an opportunity to make up with our father or mother, sister or brother. Today is the best day to ask Jesus to pour His Spirit into your heart and let the gifts of grace, mercy, and peace overflow in your life and the lives of the people you love and have loved and can love again.

Test the Lord and watch His awesome power of love, restoration and forgiveness bloom new blessing into your life…

> *To Timothy my true son in the faith:*
> *Grace, mercy and peace from God the Father and Christ Jesus our*
> *Lord.* — 1 Timothy 1:2

True and living God, Creator of the heavens and universe I praise you for my life. God, thank you for not just being a giver of grace, mercy, and peace. I thank you for being grace, mercy, and peace; because without you, Lord, I would not be able to make it through the day. As such, Father I ask that you bless me with a heart formed in your likeness of grace, mercy, and peace so that I can be a blessing to the world around me and bring glory to your name. It's in the name of my savior Jesus the Christ that I pray, amen!

## Personal Questions and Prayer Journal - Date:

What key words stuck out to you in this prayer? List three or four of those words.

List three personal things or feelings (good or not so good) that are on your heart?

Now write your own prayer using the words you wrote down and the heartfelt matters. Tell the Lord about your joy, concern, or sorrows. Let your words be known. God is listening and seeking to meet you.

# DAY 34

## Let Your Faith Grow Tall

*He replied, "Because you have so little faith. Truly I tell you, if you have faith as small as a mustard seed, you can say to this mountain, 'Move from here to there,' and it will move. Nothing will be impossible for you.* — Matthew 17:20

Sovereign Lord of the universe, speak your will and press your will through my life. In addition, I ask that you grant me with the strength, humility, discernment, patience and understanding that is needed to go higher in you. Bend my life towards your will. Water my faith with your daily reminders of affirmation. Let the scriptures soak into the soil of my soul so that I can grow to greater heights. And Lord, mold and stretch me into a vessel that can be used to bring glory to your name and blessings to your people. It's in the mighty and matchless name of Jesus the Christ that I pray. Amen.

## Personal Questions and Prayer Journal - Date:

What key words stuck out to you in this prayer? List three or four of those words.

List three personal things or feelings (good or not so good) that are on your heart?

Now write your own prayer using the words you wrote down and the heartfelt matters. Tell the Lord about your joy, concern, or sorrows. Let your words be known. God is listening and seeking to meet you.

# DAY 35

## Let God Speak Through You

*Look at the nations and watch –*
*and be utterly amazed.*
*For I am going to do something in your days*
*that you would not believe,*
*even if you were told.* — Habakkuk 1:5

Heavenly Father, I thank you for continuing to reveal yourself to me through your good and wonderful works. Show me your miracles every day. Show me the light of presence and let words of my daily prayers be pleasing to your heart. Help me to remain a witness to your awesome powers so that I may glorify your name without worry or hesitation. It's in the great and powerful name of Christ Jesus that I pray. Amen.

## Personal Questions and Prayer Journal - Date:

What key words stuck out to you in this prayer? List three or four of those words.

List three personal things or feelings (good or not so good) that are on your heart?

Now write your own prayer using the words you wrote down and the heartfelt matters. Tell the Lord about your joy, concern, or sorrows. Let your words be known. God is listening and seeking to meet you.

# DAY 36

## God's Will Is Available To You

*It is God's will that you should be sanctified: . . .* — 1 Thess. 4:3

Abba, let your will be done in me and through me. Let the effects of the cross be shown at work in me so that I may bring glory to your name and liberation to your people. God, I thank you for an unconditional love that allows me to be sanctified in you. I want you to strip away everything that is unlike you. I need you to burn out of me everything that is hindering your will in my life. And Lord set me free to be someone that you want to use today. I offer this prayer in the redeeming and healing name of Jesus. Amen.

## Personal Questions and Prayer Journal - Date:

What key words stuck out to you in this prayer? List three or four of those words.

List three personal things or feelings (good or not so good) that are on your heart?

Now write your own prayer using the words you wrote down and the heartfelt matters. Tell the Lord about your joy, concern, or sorrows. Let your words be known. God is listening and seeking to meet you.

# DAY 37

## Be Thankful For Your Open Doors

*...because a great door for effective work has opened to me, and there are many who oppose me.* — I Corinthians 16:9

Father of abundant provision, I thank you for transforming me from the inside out, so that my character can withstand the outside world. I love you, God, and I need your love every day. Please continue to talk to me daily so that I can remain on the path that you have destined me to travel. Call me forward so that I may walk with confidence in my purpose.

God, I thank you for the trials that come to make me strong.
Thank you for your will that strengthens our bond.
Thank you for the sacrifice that saved my soul.
Thank you for the love that made me whole.
Thank you for the blood that stains my heart.
Thank you for the cross that has left its mark.
Thank you for being God, the "Great I AM."
Thank you for saving me. Because of you, I am.
Thank you. Thank you. Thank you.
It's in Jesus' name that I thank you. Amen.

## Personal Questions and Prayer Journal - Date:

What key words stuck out to you in this prayer? List three or four of those words.

List three personal things or feelings (good or not so good) that are on your heart?

Now write your own prayer using the words you wrote down and the heartfelt matters. Tell the Lord about your joy, concern, or sorrows. Let your words be known. God is listening and seeking to meet you.

# DAY 38

## Lifting The Right Name

*hallowed be Your name.* — Matthew 6:9 b

King Jesus! Lord of all! My Amazing Savior! Help me to improve my relationship and understanding of who you are so that I can maintain the holiness of your name in the presence of my friends and enemies. Show me how to live with a reverence for your name that promotes wonder and an appealing fragrance to all. Forgive me for using your name. Forgive me for not lifting your name in situations that required peace and loving understanding. Lead me back to reverencing your name as the source of healing, deliverance, life and joy. Lead me back to lifting up your name as the standard of light and salt. And place your name on my heart so that I can share it with the people that need your love, hope, and salvation. It's in your mighty and unmatchable name that I lift this prayer. Amen!

## Personal Questions and Prayer Journal - Date:

What key words stuck out to you in this prayer? List three or four of those words.

List three personal things or feelings (good or not so good) that are on your heart?

Now write your own prayer using the words you wrote down and the heartfelt matters. Tell the Lord about your joy, concern, or sorrows. Let your words be known. God is listening and seeking to meet you.

# DAY 39

## Finishing Strong

*Let perseverance finish its work so that you may be mature and complete, not lacking anything.* — James 1:4

My Strong and Amazing Lord, please be with me today and let your discernment and love fall fresh over me so that I may accomplish a good day's work. Keep me close when I forget to put on my crown of faith. Cover me when I lack the wisdom and discernment. And correct me with your prompting when I'm just plain lazy and fall short of the mark. Lord, I want to get it right today, be a blessing today, remain aligned in your will today and that's why I need your help because I'm noting without you, especially today. Set me on fire and use me. I am ready to start this day, and I want to finish it strong in Jesus' name. Amen.

## Personal Questions and Prayer Journal - Date:

What key words stuck out to you in this prayer? List three or four of those words.

List three personal things or feelings (good or not so good) that are on your heart?

Now write your own prayer using the words you wrote down and the heartfelt matters. Tell the Lord about your joy, concern, or sorrows. Let your words be known. God is listening and seeking to meet you.

# DAY 40

## His Light Is Your Light

*You are the light of the world. A town built on a hill cannot be hidden.*
— Matthew 5:14

Brilliant and Beautiful Lord, let your stunning light shine in my life so that I may reflect the awesomeness of your love and joy to everyone that I meet. Let your light of freedom be seen in my actions, my conversations, and my desires. Open my heart so that I can receive the goodness of your blessing. Fill my cup so that I can be an overflowing blessing to the empty hands that seeks love, comfort, provisions, and friendship. It's in the shining name of Jesus that I pray. Amen.

## Personal Questions and Prayer Journal - Date:

What key words stuck out to you in this prayer? List three or four of those words.

List three personal things or feelings (good or not so good) that are on your heart?

Now write your own prayer using the words you wrote down and the heartfelt matters. Tell the Lord about your joy, concern, or sorrows. Let your words be known. God is listening and seeking to meet you.

# ACKNOWLEDGEMENTS

To my Lord God, my Savior Jesus Christ, and the Holy Spirit, thank you for believing in me.

To my wonderful son, Khaleed A. Case – you are so amazing and I am honored to be your father.

To my father, Jerome R. Case – thank you for encouraging me to live out my calling.

To my brother, Marcellus Sawyer – thank for allowing me to be a spiritual resource in your life.

To my pastor, Cynthia L. Hale – your belief in me helped to stir up the gifts in my life. Thank you for the many opportunities to develop in ministry and for interceding on my behalf.

To my pastor, Carl H. McRae – I am so grateful for the care, encouragement and love that you have supplied while allowing me to develop in my apostolic and prophetic calling.

To my amazing surrogate mother, Theresa Dunwood – your friendship, love, compassion, encouragement and private prayers over my life have carried and lifted me through times of adversity.

To my thoughtful friend, Keith J. Hammond – I appreciate your supportive friendship and ministry collaboration. Thank you for praying powerful declarations over my life.

To my amazing friend, Kewon M. Foster – your support of my ministry gifts have been invaluable. Thank you for praying for me and trusting me.

www.ingramcontent.com/pod-product-compliance
Lightning Source LLC
LaVergne TN
LVHW021523080426
835509LV00018B/2632